But Seek Ye First

30 DAYS in MATTHEW 6:33

DANNY GODDARD

dustjacket

©2018 by Danny Goddard

©2018 Dust Jacket Press
But Seek Ye First: 30 Days in Matthew 6:33

ISBN: 978-1-947671-09-6

Dust Jacket Press
P.O. Box 721243
Oklahoma City, OK 73172
www.dustjacket.com

Ordering information for print editions:
Quantity sales. Special discounts are available on quantity purchases by corporations, associations, and others. For details, contact the Dust Jacket Press address above.

Individual sales. Dust Jacket Press publications are available through most bookstores. They can also be ordered directly from Dust Jacket: Tel: (800) 495-0192; Email: info@dustjacket.com; www.dustjacket.com

Dust Jacket logos are registered trademarks of Dust Jacket Press, Inc.

All Scripture quotations, unless otherwise indicated, are taken from New International Version.

Scripture quotations marked " NIV" are taken from the Holy Bible, New International Version® NIV®. Copyright ©1973, 1978, 1984, 2011 by Biblica, Inc. Used by permission of Zondervan. All rights reserved worldwide. www.zondervan.com. The " NIV" and "New International Version" are trademarks registered in the United States Patent and Trademark Office by Biblica, Inc.

Scripture quotations marked (NLT) are taken from the Holy Bible, New Living Translation, copyright © 1996, 2004, 2007 by Tyndale House Foundation. Used by permission of Tyndale House Publishers, Inc., Carol Stream, Illinois 60188. All rights reserved.

Cover & Interior Design: D.E. West / ZAQ Designs and Dust Jacket Creative Services

Printed in the United States of America

🐦 dustjacket
www.dustjacket.com

In loving memory of
Dr. Stan Toler,
my fellow minister, my friend.
I learned so much from his life
and I continue to learn
through his books.

CONTENTS

Dedication III

Introduction.. VII

1—But 1

2—I Want to be a God-Seeker! 3

3—God First!..5

4—Praying Properly..7

5—Worriers to Weapons 9

6—But Now Jesus Has Moved In!.................................11

7—May I Remind You?...13

8—Love of My Life...15

9—"No Cows in Tommy's Room!" 17

10—Let the Walls Fall!...19

11—Putting God First in My Prayer Life 21

12—Putting God First in Tithing..................................23

13—Putting God First in Compassion 25

14—"TC in '73!"...27

15—"Yes, Lord" 29

16—Surrendering Without Giving Up..........................31

17—Sunday, Still the Lord's Day!.................................33

18—God's Call 35

19—Living the Sanctified Life......................................37

20—Where is God in Your Spiritual Life? 39

21—Where is God in Your Home? 41

22—Where is God in Your Future? 43

23—Where is God in Your Problem-Solving? 45

24—First in Finance 47

25—Facing Our Fears 49

26—For the Birds! 51

27—Following Jesus 53

28—Why Worry? 55

29—Faith 57

30—Following Jesus All the Way Home 59

Notes 61

INTRODUCTION

But seek ye first the kingdom of God,
and his righteousness; and all these things
shall be added unto you.
(Matthew 6:33, KJV)

We called it the "live-in." The teens of the church moved into the parsonage and lived with Sandie, our son, and me for a week. The girls slept in sleeping bags on the floor in one room and the guys in another. Volunteers from church transported them to and from several different schools each day. If one had an afternoon doctor's appointment or sports practice, we all went as a family.

Being the leader of our teen ministry, my wife was in charge of the live-in. After dinner each evening, Sandie would lead the group in devotions and she had prayerfully landed on Matthew 6:33 as the theme for the week. Night after night, she talked to those kids about seeking God and

His Kingdom first in their lives. Matthew 6:33 had been a favorite of mine, ever since my former pastor, Dr. Jim Diehl, once shared with me that it was his life verse.

I really felt that our church was on the verge of revival. If only a few in that congregation would just "let go and let God," I believed the Holy Spirit would be poured out like never seen before. What a burden I had to see that happen, driving me to my knees, believing God for His Will to be accomplished.

Inspired by the devotional thoughts I heard at our teen event throughout the week, I felt led to preach from Matthew 6:33 on the following Sunday morning. Although we did have a few seekers, I didn't feel that we had the spiritual breakthrough that was needed.

After church that Sunday morning, I told Sandie that I felt like they "just didn't get it," and I was tempted to revisit that same text again in the evening service. She encouraged me to do whatever I felt God was leading me to do. So, that afternoon, instead of my usual "Nazarene nap," I spent time in prayer and Bible study, putting together a different message from the same text. That night, I again preached Matthew 6:33. There were more seekers.

But throughout the following week, I couldn't sense a release from that middle verse of the Sermon on the Mount. So the next Sunday morning and evening, I preached two more sermons from Matthew 6:33, and the same the next Sunday and the next! As a matter of fact, before I felt the

Holy Spirit's approval to move on to another text and topic, I preached twenty-seven consecutive sermons from Matthew 6:33!

I've always asked the congregation to stand for the reading of the Scripture and it wasn't long before they were no longer reading, but quoting! God began to speak, and we saw spiritual victory in the lives of our people in so many different ways.

In a recent telephone conversation with my good friend, Dr. Jim Thrower, I mentioned this experience and his response was that maybe I should put those messages into a book (Something my wife had also suggested). Even more recently, Evangelist Jeremiah Bolich also advised me to put my thoughts into devotional form. So, prompted by their encouragement, with support from my wife, here's the book. My appreciation to Sandie who has proof-read this manuscript more than once.

In his book, Powering Up, Dr. Jack Graham mentions several tasks that are important for him. He then wrote, "But according to the priority of Scripture, I am first to seek the kingdom of God. And as I approach my day each morning, I find it extremely helpful to keep this truth in mind."[1] For Pastor Graham, seeking God first is to be a daily thing, as it should be for each of us.

Therefore, along with the twenty-seven preached outlines, I've added a few newer ones to make enough devotionals for thirty days, a month. My prayer is that what started with the Holy Spirit's outpouring on some teenagers in a live-in will touch your heart and encourage your own spiritual growth with thirty days in Matthew 6:33. It simply comes down to this—Jesus is all we need and nothing else matters.

Danny Goddard
New Castle, Indiana

1

But strive first for the kingdom of God and his
righteousness, and all these things will
be given to you as well.
(Matthew 6:33, NRSV)

But ...

Jesus looked at His disciples and was anything but
pleased. They were worrying and fretting over everyday needs—food, clothes, shelter. Jesus addressed this
in Matthew 6:19-22 and then He spoke one powerful
word, *"But!"*

"But" is a conjunction. It implies change. "Then His
disciples came to Him ... saying, 'Lord, save us! ... *But* He
said to them, 'Why are you fearful, O you of little faith?'
Then He arose and rebuked the winds and the sea, and
there was a great calm." (Matthew 8:25-26) "Then the spirit cried out ... and came out of him. And he became as one
dead ... *But* Jesus took him by the hand and lifted him up,
and he arose." (Mark 9:26-27) "Peter was therefore kept
in prison, *but* constant prayer was offered to God for him
by the church." (Acts 12:5) The conjunction *"but"* implies
something's about to happen—for the better!

In Matthew 6:33, Jesus makes some suggestions for His followers …

1. Instead of worry, trust!

The verb tense tells us this is a command with no act of completion. It's a new way of living.

2. Instead of contentment, try commitment!

Jesus wants us fully committed to Him. That means we want His will and His way rather than our own.

3. Instead of selfishness, live a life of selflessness.

The disciples wondered where 5,000 people might get lunch. Jesus replied, *"You* feed them!"* (Matthew 14:16)

4. Instead of second place, determine to be first!

Deuteronomy 6:5 tells us to love God with our entire being. It's all about Him! So someone did you wrong long ago, *but* Jesus wants you to forgive! You're struggling with the bills, *but* Jesus wants to provide! Discouraging news has come from the doctor, *but* Jesus wants you to just trust Him!

The disciples easily got caught up in stress and worry and discouragement, however, Jesus used the powerful little word, *"But!"* Aren't you glad there's a better way to live?

As you pray today, ask God to show you
what needs to be replaced in your life for the better.

2

But seek first the kingdom of God and his righteousness,
and all these things will be added to you.
(Matthew 6:33, ESV)

I Want to Be a God-Seeker!

When I was a kid, I wanted to be a doctor. Then I heard how many years of school were required and I quickly changed my mind. Some want to be successful without hard work. Some want to lose weight without exercise or a proper diet. We want a quick fix. We want to win the lottery. We want to drink something to make us skinny and we want to waltz into a high-paying job. But someone once told me, "There's no such thing as a free lunch!"

The same things apply to our spiritual lives. We want the joy of Jesus, we want to walk with the Spirit, and we want to get to heaven when we die. Jesus says in Matthew 6:33, if we want His hand upon our lives, we must become God-seekers.

1. To be a God-seeker means I want Him!

Some only want what God can do for them. Jesus once told a crowd of followers, "you are looking for me, not because you saw signs, but because you ate your fill of the loaves." (John 6:26)

2. To be a God-seeker means I want to be filled with Him!

We can only be filled after we've emptied ourselves of ourselves. My mind must be filled with His Word. (Psalm 1:1-2) My mouth must be filled with His song. (Ephesians 5:19) My methods must be filled with His will. (Matthew 7:24)

3. To be a God-seeker means I want to be like Him!

I want to pray like Jesus prayed. (Luke 6:12) I want to think like Jesus thought. (Philippians 2:1-5) I want to live like Jesus lived. (1 John 2:6) One of my favorite Scriptures is Acts 4:13, "Now when they saw the boldness of Peter and John, and perceived that they were uneducated and untrained men, they marveled. And they realized that they had been with Jesus."

Have you been with Jesus? If so, it should show.

As you pray today, ask God to help you to become a God-seeker.

3

But seek first his kingdom and his righteousness,
and all these things will be given to you as well.
(Matthew 6:33, NIV)

God First!

I heard a man testify in church on a Wednesday night
that he had told his friend how he always tries to put
God first in his life. In reply, his believer-buddy admitted,
"I don't put God first!"

The Apostle Paul said that there is one thing that he
does (and it's a two-fold thing), he forgets the past and
reaches to the future. (Philippians 3:13) *"One thing"* is a
phrase that should be important to every Christian ...

To the rich young ruler, Jesus pointed out, "you still
lack *one thing* ..." (Luke 18:22) To forever busy Martha, Jesus said: *"One thing* is needful ..." (Luke 10:42) The healed
blind man publicly professed, *"One thing* I know ..." (John
9:25) Even the psalmist declared *"One thing* have I desired
of the Lord ..." (Psalm 27:4)

We absolutely must devote ourselves to only one thing
in this life and that one thing is Jesus! Why not make that
our goal for the days ahead? Let's put God first in all our ac-
tivities! Pay His tithe before the bills! Go to Sunday School

before sleeping-in! Let's invite our friends to church before inviting them to everything else! Read the Bible before reading the newspaper! Pray before making decisions. Practice going to church on a regular basis!

Tall charge? I'm convinced that the only way this kind of change will ever take place in our lives is if we are sanctified "wholly!" (1 Thessalonians 5:23) The NIV says "through and through."

Dr. William Greathouse wrote, *"The crowning work of the Holy Spirit is entire sanctification or Christian perfection."*[1] God wants you and me to be both saved *and* sanctified, two definite works of God's grace.

To be saved, we repent of our sins. To be sanctified, we consecrate ourselves to God. We surrender ourselves fully to the Lord and we allow God the throne of our lives. In return, He will direct each and every step on our journey with Jesus. Could full surrender be what is lacking in you?

As you pray today, ask God to point out what may be keeping Him from being first in your life.

4

But seek first the kingdom of God and His righteousness,
and all these things shall be added to you.
(Matthew 6:33, NKJV)

Praying Properly

The disciples were praying improper prayers because they didn't have proper concerns (Matthew 6:25-32) Verse 33 clearly presents the appropriate concern. Rather than asking for food, clothes, and other such things, they should have been praying, "Thy Kingdom come, Thy will be done!"

But let's not come down too hard on those disciples because there may be a few places where we might not be so proper. We pray for power, rather than His Presence. We pray for feelings, rather than faith. We pray for here, instead of the hereafter. So how do we acquire the proper mindset?

1. The practice.

There are only two ways to live: Seeking God and His things, or seeking self and my things. The problem comes in seeking the wrong things. We must remember that the word "seek" implies, "searching until you find!"

2. The priority.

It's okay to be concerned about things that we need, but our priorities must forever be in the proper order. God must be first, no questions asked! This prompts a checklist: Do I desire to spend time with Him? Do I long to worship Him? Do I ask Him for wisdom and for direction? Do I seek Him on a daily basis?

3. The promise.

The promise is plainly presented in Matthew 6:33. If we put God first, He vows to meet our needs. The Weymouth Translation reads, "And these things shall be given you in addition." Three times Jesus was tempted by the devil but each time our Lord failed to give-in. Eugene Peterson translates Matthew 4:11, "Angels came and took care of Jesus' needs." (*The Message*)

But is God able to do that for us? For me? For you? Paul wrote the Christians at Ephesus, "Now to Him who is able to do exceedingly abundantly above all that we ask or think, according to the power that works in us." (Ephesians 3:20) Yes, He can, and He will!

As you pray today, ask God to show
you the changes that are needed before you can
acquire the Mind of Christ.

5

Seek the Kingdom of God above all else, and live
righteously, and he will give you everything you need.
(Matthew 6:33, NLT)

Worries to Weapons

It was a cold December Wednesday on Windy Hill
Road in Marietta, Georgia. After shivering under a
cemetery canopy, we returned to our cars. I was having a
hard time leaving my Dad in a hole in the ground.

Daddy often bailed me out of trouble, mostly financial.
He had paid my bills, assumed payments on my motor-
cycle, and even retrieved the $20 I had foolishly put down
on a new car. And now, at age 22, I was leaving my Dad, as
well as my home.

Two days later, with less than $30 in my pocket,
I headed to Nashville to begin my college career. Who
would bail me out now? It was my time to put Matthew
6:33 into practice and to turn my worries into weapons ...

1. Worry is a tool of Satan!

The disciples were worried. Peter reminded Jesus how
he had left all to follow Him (Mark 10:28) and Jesus
warned him that the devil wanted to sift him as wheat.
(Luke 22:31)

2. The Devil loves to exaggerate!

Satan loves to blow things up bigger than they are. He exaggerated to the spies (Numbers 13:31-33), to Gideon (Judges 6:14-15), to Elijah (1 Kings 19:10-18), to Elisha (2 Kings 6:15-17), to Judas (Matthew 27:3-5), and even to Jesus. (Matthew 27:46)

3. The opposite of worry is trust!

God knows that all we need is to trust Him. In *The Cycle of Victorious Living,* Dr. Earl Lee defined "trust" as to "lean hard."[1] It's time to "lean hard" on our Creator.

4. We are expected to fight in the battle!

Like it or not, we are involved in spiritual warfare (Ephesians 6:10-18) where one's posture is important on the battlefield. A worrisome posture is head down, body bent over. But Hebrews 12:12-14 tells us to straighten up and strengthen our knees!

5. There's always victory in Jesus!

More than a song, it's reality for the Christian! Let's heed the words of Matthew 6:33, turning our worries into weapons!

As you pray today, ask God to deliver
you from worry.

6

But seek ye first the kingdom of God, and his
righteousness; and all these things
shall be added unto you.
(Matthew 6:33, KJV)

But Now Jesus Has Moved In!

I remember a church that had become an eyesore in the community. With a fresh vision, friends of ours accepted that pastorate and soon there were new doors, windows, lights. Everything was different. New leadership had moved in!

At 19, my life was a mess! Sin was in my heart and I was headed in the wrong direction, but on a Sunday night, I responded to the Gospel. Because Jesus had moved in, several changes took place ...

1. He changed the way I talk.

Our Lord said, "those things which proceed out of the mouth come from the heart, and they defile a man." (Matthew 15:18) Jesus helped me to replace some negative and unchristian words with those that are positive and wholesome.

2. He changed the way I walk.

In days past, I went my own way, practiced my own agenda, but then Jesus moved in! "He who says he abides

in Him ought himself also to walk just as He walked."
(1 John 2:6)

3. He changed the way I listen.

My only desire had been to satisfy king self, that is, until Jesus moved in! "Your ears shall hear a word behind you, saying, 'This is the way, walk in it.'" (Isaiah 30:21)

4. He changed the way I think.

I used to think negatively and small, but then Jesus moved in! He has helped me to see that God can do anything. Paul encouraged believers to have a positive mindset. (Philippians 4:8) I began to see that, come what may, God can take care of it!

5. He changed the way I see.

I once had a negative viewpoint of life, but then Jesus moved in! Having no other explanation for his healing, the blind man exclaimed, "One thing I know: that though I was blind, now I see." (John 9:25)

Where are you in your journey with Jesus? Get into Matthew 6:33 and start seeking God with your entire being. Once Jesus moves in, all will be different!

As you pray today, ask God to help
you become more like Jesus.

7

But strive first for the kingdom of God and his
righteousness, and all these things will be
given to you as well.
(Matthew 6:33, NRSV)

May I Remind You?

Matthew 6:33 calls us to be God-seekers. That is, God and His Will and Way should take precedence in our lives. To prevent the enemy from strapping blinders on us, we need some spiritual reminders along the way.

1. May I remind you of your attitude?

As we grow older, we make adjustments. We need to learn how to accept change, even if it messes with our personal preference. We need to become more forgiving, even though someone may have hurt us long ago. We should discover how to delegate authority, allowing younger Christians to assume roles of leadership in church. And our faith should be forever increasing as we scoot farther out on that tiny limb of faith.

It's easy for a child of God to become hardened, callused, and bitter, even looking down our righteous noses at others. For this reason, Paul discusses having the Mind of Christ in Philippians 2.

2. May I remind you of your spirit?

General Booth of the Salvation Army said, "The tendency of fire is to go out; watch the fire on the altar of your heart." When Jesus entered our hearts, He lit a fire! Paul admonished young preacher-boy Timothy to always be about fanning the flame. (2 Timothy 1:6)

3. May I remind you of your walk?

One of my favorite Scriptures is 1 John 2:6, "He who says he abides in Him ought himself also to walk just as He walked." My son has been accused of walking the way I walk, and some have said that I walk the way my Dad walked. We need to walk the way Jesus did.

It has been suggested there are three steps to a godly walk. First there's communication. Instead of worrying and criticizing, pray. Next there's compassion, seeing people through the eyes of a kindhearted Christ. Then there is commitment, keeping our sacrifice on the altar.

All of this is wrapped up in Matthew 6:33, a great reminder as to what it means to seek Him first.

As you pray today, ask God to remind you on a daily basis what it means to be a Spirit-filled Christian.

8

But seek first the kingdom of God and his righteousness,
and all these things will be added to you.
(Matthew 6:33, ESV)

Love of My Life

Knowing I'm not fond of water, a very young Tommy asked me, as we stood in the backyard pool, "Why will you go swimming with me?" My answer, "Because I love you." When Sandie and I were dating, she would watch late-night TV reruns of *The Honeymooners* with me. Why? Only because she loved me. Whenever we love someone, we seem to be able to muster up an interest in their favorites.

A multitude had gathered around Jesus of Nazareth. He preached an inspiring sermon that day, eventually addressing a personal relationship with

God. In the center of the Sermon on the Mount is Matthew 6:33. It's a love affair!

Peter ended up denying our Lord on three occasions, after which, Jesus was crucified, buried, and raised from the dead. Returning to the shore after fishing, Peter and his friends found the resurrected Christ cooking breakfast on the beach! Jesus asks Peter, "Do you love Me more than these?" (John 21:15)

We are not told of His gestures or to what He may have pointed. What did He mean?

1. He may have meant, "Do you love Me more than you love these, your friends?" Peter was mighty fond of his buddies and there's nothing wrong with that, as long as Jesus is Number One.

2. He may have meant, "Do you love Me more than you love these boats and nets and catches of fish?" Fishing had been Peter's livelihood. There's nothing wrong with enjoying what we do, unless it comes before Jesus.

3. He may have meant, "Do you love Me more than these other disciples love me" Peter had once boasted that if the others fell away, he would remain faithful. (Mark 14:29) But we cannot watch others—we must keep our eyes on Him.

The truth is, Peter was incapable of loving Jesus supremely without being Spirit-filled, something that happened for him on the Day of Pentecost. The question I must ask myself is this: Is Jesus Christ the Love of my life?

As you pray today, ask God to help you
to make Him the Love of your life.

9

But seek first his kingdom and his righteousness,
and all these things will be given to you as well.
(Matthew 6:33, NIV)

"No Cows in Tommy's Room!"

Jesus began His Sermon on the Mount with the
"Beatitudes." ("Blessed are the poor in spirit," "those
who mourn," "the meek," etc.) The key word is *"blessed" or*
"happy," a term that described joy for gods! Only the Christian can enjoy *"godly happiness!"*

Randal Denny wrote, "The greatest deterrent to the
unconverted onlooker is the Christian who has not formed
the habit of happiness … He is not suggesting, 'Live like
this and you will become a Christian.' The Master is saying,
'Because you are a Christian, live like this.'"[1] But we have
been robbed of our happiness by a worrisome attitude.

Most two-year olds fear "monsters" in their rooms,
but for our Tommy, it was cows! Sandie was working in
the kitchen one day when she heard little Tommer com-
ing quickly down the hall from his room where he had
been playing. He asked his Mom, *"Cows in Tommy's room?"*
She assured him that there were no cows in his room. As
he made his way back down the hall, she heard him say-

ing under his breath, *"No cows in Tommy's room! No cows in Tommy's room!"* Then, just to be safe, he added, *"No giraffes!"*

Just as ridiculous are the things over which we worry! Norman Vincent Peale said worry is "an unhealthy and destructive mental habit. You were not born with the worry habit. You acquired it. And because you can change any habit and any acquired attitude, you can cast worry from your mind."[2] Jesus gave three arguments for not worrying ...

The birds argument. (v. 26) Birds are not served on a silver platter but are fed regularly by their heavenly Father.

The growth argument. (v. 27) The same Greek word is used for growth or maturity, age or size. The short Palestinians envied the tall Roman soldiers.

The lilies argument. (v. 28-29) A flower's beauty comes from the inside. A king could wear fancy robes on the outside, but still have sin in his heart! (v. 30-32) Five times in ten verses, Jesus says, *"Do not worry!"* He would have never said it had worry been incurable! (v. 25, 33)

As you pray today, ask God to help
you with your attitude.

10

But seek first the kingdom of God and His righteousness,
and all these things shall be added to you.
(Matthew 6:33, NKJV)

Let the Walls Fall!

The number one purpose of God is His Kingdom. In February 1996, I had a glimpse of the Kingdom, a picture of heaven on earth. I was one of 39,000 ministers attending the Promise Keepers Clergy Conference in Atlanta's Georgia Dome. The focus of the convention was, "Let the Walls Come Down!"

1. The walls of worship were the first to fall!

We can worship God anywhere! After one of the evening services, some preachers in a subway under the streets of Atlanta began to sing "Amazing Grace." It quickly caught on to others, until a mass of ministers awaiting their trains were worshiping God underneath the city!

We can worship God with anyone. Several times in that meeting, we got into prayer groups with those around us. I, a Nazarene, prayed that weekend with a Catholic, a Southern Baptist, and an Episcopalian.

We can worship God any way! I saw hands raised, hands down. Some were quiet, others shouted. Several danced in the aisles. All were worshiping Jesus.

2. The walls of denominationalism were next to crumble!

Paul wrote that "there may be no divisions among you" (1 Corinthians 1:10) After a moving message by Max Lucado on the divided Church, we were asked to seek out and apologize to brothers or sisters of other denominations. I heard one man shouting, "A Presbyterian pastor here?" I witnessed another preacher saying to a Harley rider, "I've judged you by what you wear and I'm sorry!"

3. The walls of racism were the last to go!

Hebrews 12:14 speaks of "peace with all men." Clergy of various colors voiced their apologies, some out loud from the balconies. A Native American next to me hugged me, saying, "I love you, my brother."

All of this was followed by Steve Green leading a 100-voice preacher-choir: *"Let the walls come down; Let the walls come down; Let the walls that divide us and hide us come down."*

This is the Kingdom of God. Are you part of the Kingdom?

⸙ ———— • ———— ⸙

As you pray today, ask God to bring
down some walls in your life.

11

Seek the Kingdom of God above all else, and live
righteously, and he will give you everything you need.
(Matthew 6:33, NLT)

Putting God First in
My Prayer Life

No words are more fundamental to Christianity
than these words of Christ, "Seek ye first!" Anything less than putting God first is idolatry.

Dr. Tony Evans wrote, "Idolatry is worshiping anyone or anything other than God, putting something else
ahead of God."[1] We sometimes wonder, "Why am I having
such a struggle in my devotional life? Why does it seem
to be a chore to even pray?" Could it be that God is not
Number One?

If we put God first in our lives, prayer will be natural. What is more natural than conversation with those we
love? For the many years Sandie and I lived away from her
Mom and Dad, we talked with them on the phone weekly.
Those years were before cell phones and we had to pay long
distance charges. Every Sunday night we talked with her
parents for one solid hour. We called one week, they called

the next, we split the bill and we kept watch on the clock. We did that because to the four of us, it was worth it.

The same is true of God. If He really is first, if He really does mean more than anything, if He really is our number one priority, we want to stay in His company. Therefore, prayer should be as natural to us as eating and sleeping.

The Apostle Paul admonished the believers at Thessalonica to "Pray without ceasing." (1 Thessalonians 5:17) Is that realistic? How can that be done? I have learned that if I leave my morning prayer without an end, without an "Amen," I can leave my prayer line open throughout the day. Then when that car is crossing the center line in front of me and heading in my direction, I don't have to go through the "Dear gracious Heavenly Father" introduction to my prayer. Instead, I yell, "Help me, Jesus!" I'm already in a state of conversation with my Father because I never closed my prayer.

Let's keep God first by making Him Number One in our prayer lives.

As you pray today, ask God to help you strengthen your prayer life.

12

But seek ye first the kingdom of God,
and his righteousness; and all these things
shall be added unto you.
(Matthew 6:33, KJV)

Putting God First in Tithing

We've discussed how God should be first in our prayer lives. If we put God first, prayer will be natural. But if we put God first, tithing will be simple.

One of my dedicated church members invited an unchurched friend to attend with him, and he did, for several weeks. Everything preached was brand new to him, especially my Sunday morning message on tithing. As I was explaining how Christians are to bring ten percent of their paycheck to God, our new attendee nearly snapped his neck as he turned to his Christian friend beside him and asked, "Do *you* do that?" The response, of course, was, "Yes."

To give a tenth of one's payday to the church, and then to give anything extra in beyond-the-tithe giving is pretty bazaar to the world without Christ. For the Christian, however, tithing is a joyful part of worship.

In Old Testament days, God was a bit perturbed with the Israelites for offering Him lame and blind animals, much less than what they offered the local officials. God was even so bold as to accuse them of being robbers and thieves if they did not bring tithes *and* offerings. (Malachi 3:8-10)

What does that mean for us today? It means that if I am a child of God, I am going to put Him first in all areas of my life, including tithes and offerings.

Don't say you can't afford to tithe. If you have a dollar, you have a dime for the Lord. If you have any amount of money at all, a tenth belongs to the One Who gave His life for you. Systematic tithing and giving beyond the tithe is a good way to put God first in our lives. Jesus teaches us in Matthew 6:33 that, if we keep God first, even in our finances, He will take care of all of our needs.

<hr />

As you pray today, ask God to help you to become a faithful tither as well as a generous giver.

13

But strive first for the kingdom of God and his
righteousness, and all these things will be
given to you as well.
(Matthew 6:33, NRSV)

Putting God First in Compassion

Putting God first means God should be Number One in our prayer lives. If we put God first, prayer will be natural. It also means to tithe and to give beyond, because if we put God first, tithing will be simple. But there's one more powerful truth: If we put God first, people will become important.

The Bible teaches us that human beings are the crown of creation. We are made in the image of Almighty God and therefore, we have a special relationship with the King of kings and Lord of lords. That means we should place value where He does, on people. The Apostle Paul wrote, "Let nothing be done through selfish ambition or conceit, but in lowliness of mind let each esteem others better than himself. Let each of you look out not only for his own interests, but also for the interests of others." (Philippians 2:3-4)

Do people mean that much to us? Do we see others the way Jesus saw them? "But when He saw the multitudes, He was moved with compassion for them, because they were weary and scattered, like sheep having no shepherd." (Matthew 9:36) Jesus went on to tell His disciples to pray that the Lord of the harvest would send out the needed workers. Those boys evidently prayed, because the next few verses tell us that they were the very ones who were sent out to bring in the harvest.

I once heard a nonbeliever say, "I've seen Christians in the church who don't live any better than I!" We can't speak for everyone else at the church-house, but we can speak for ourselves. I, for one, want to keep God first by making people a priority in my life. I want to view everyone the same way Jesus viewed them. I want to have a heart that goes out to the lost, the less fortunate, and the ones who are hurting. What about you?

As you pray today, ask God to help you
to see people with the compassion of Christ.

14

But seek first the kingdom of God and his righteousness,
and all these things will be added to you.
(Matthew 6:33, ESV)

"TC in '73!"

It was late 1972. Although I was nineteen, I was about one-month old as a believer. In those days, I was taking evening classes at the Atlanta Professional Academy of Commercial Art with hopes of some day being "discovered" and landing a job as a full time cartoonist. Wouldn't be wonderful to work for Disney and draw Mickey Mouse for a living? My pastor at Atlanta First Church of the Nazarene, Dr. Bennet Dudney, was well aware of my dream and ambitions and he decided to give me an opportunity to at least use my talents for the church.

Pastor Dudney asked me to design several posters to be displayed around the church facilities bearing the teaser, *"TC in 73."* For the last few weeks of the year, church attendees wondered what this message could possibly mean.

Finally, 1973 came and Dr. Dudney revealed the mysterious message in his New Year's sermon, *"TC in 73—Total Commitment in 1973!"* That's what Jesus was talking about in Matthew 6:33! To seek God first was another way of describing total commitment. We must allow Him to be first and foremost by our full surrender.

I think most of us would say that we are committed to the Lord Jesus, but how many of us could add the word "totally?" Are you totally committed to His will and His way? Are you totally committed to your church and its ministries? Are you totally committed to devotions and a life of prayer?

Christianity is not for the fainthearted and those with a shallow dedication. It's *"TC in 73"* or 2018 or 2020 or whatever year it might be. Paul put it this way, "I beseech you therefore, brethren, by the mercies of God, that you present your bodies a living sacrifice, holy, acceptable to God, which is your reasonable service. And do not be conformed to this world, but be transformed by the renewing of your mind, that you may prove what is that good and acceptable and perfect will of God." (Romans 12:1-2)

⋅⋅⋅ ❧ ⋅⋅⋅

As you pray today, ask God to help you
live a life of total commitment.

15

But seek first his kingdom and his righteousness,
and all these things will be given to you as well.
(Matthew 6:33, NIV)

"Yes, Lord"

God called the prophet Jonah to go preach to the people in the terribly wicked city of Nineveh, but instead, Jonah found a ship going to Tarshish, and the Bible adds, "away from the presence of the LORD." (Jonah 1:3) Everything for the prophet was downhill from there: God sent a storm on the sea, Jonah was pitched overboard by the frightened mariners who had been affected by his sin, and he was quickly swallowed by a fish that was large and in charge!

You know the story, how the prophet finally prayed from the belly of the whale and that fish spewed the prophet onto dry land. (A backslidden preacher is enough to make anyone seasick, even a whale!) Jonah then cried to the Lord, pledging his allegiance and asking Him where He wanted him to go. It should be no surprise that God's Call for Jonah was the same as before, to go preach to the people in the terribly wicked city of Nineveh. (Jonah 3:2)

Jonah would have saved himself and others lots of trouble and heartache, had he only obeyed God the first time! When God originally directed him to Nineveh, he should have just answered, "Yes, Lord!" In putting God first, as presented in Matthew 6:33, that should always be our answer, as well.

Just after I became a Christian, I wanted to order a name plate for my desk but I had to decide what to put on it. How about "Danny Goddard?" Or perhaps, "Danny E. Goddard?" What about "D.E. Goddard?" Any of those would work and be appropriate. But after careful thought, I made my decision and ordered the nameplate which is still displayed in my study to this day. It simply says, "YES, LORD." Seeing it almost every day, it's a constant reminder that whatever God tells me to do or wherever He tells me to go, my answer will forever be the same, "Yes, Lord." What is *your* answer?

———————⚬———————

As you pray today, ask God to help you
to always hear and be obedient to His Voice.

16

But seek first the kingdom of God and His righteousness,
and all these things shall be added to you.
(Matthew 6:33, NKJV)

Surrendering Without Giving Up

Most come to church to be lifted and encouraged, yet it is there that we are told to "surrender" to Jesus! Some in those very pews are about to give up, throwing in the towel, even spiritually. The Galatians did, (Galatians 1:6) as did the Ephesians. (Revelation 2:4) The Jews were going back to Judaism. (Hebrews 6) For many, it appears to be much too difficult to follow Jesus.

But the life of full surrender to Christ is a positive thing, not negative! It's not about giving up but rather giving in. Amidst the problems, pressures, and predicaments, we can surrender to the Lord Jesus and rise above it all. It's surrendering the Matthew 6:33 way ...

1. It means an attitude that's prayerful.

The disciples worried over several things when all Jesus wanted them to do was seek the will of God.

2. It means a life that's peaceful.

When we're living within our own wills, there's stress, worry, anxiety. The surrendered life is a life of trust. The cheerleader falls backwards into the arms of his or her peers—that's trust. In Acts 12, Peter was sleeping like a baby in prison on what could have been his night of execution—that's trust.

3. It means a God Who's powerful.

To the disciples, food and clothing were big deals. (Matthew 6:11, 19, 25) In every situation of life, Jesus says to trust God!

Moses and the Israelites were backed up against the Red Sea with the Egyptians gaining on them, yet God opened the waters and swallowed the enemy! David faced Goliath with only a sling and a few stones and God used a shepherd boy to slay a giant! Three Hebrew teenagers were thrown into a fiery furnace, yet instead of three in the fire, there were four, including the preincarnate Christ! Paul and Silas were in a Philippian jail facing death, yet at midnight they sang hymns until God set them free!

What are you facing in your life right now? Don't give up—give in! Surrender totally to Jesus.

As you pray today, ask God to show you the thing or things you need to surrender to Him.

17

Seek the Kingdom of God above all else, and live
righteously, and he will give you everything you need.
(Matthew 6:33, NLT)

Sunday, Still the Lord's Day!

D.L. Moody said, "Show me a nation that has given up the Sabbath and I will show you a nation
that has the seeds of decay."[1]

I grew up thinking it was a sin to play golf. On the way
to Sunday School, we'd stop at a traffic light next to East
Lake Country Club. Watching the golfers, my Dad would
say, "I'd hate to be in their shoes on Judgment Day." Daddy
felt their sin was not in playing golf but in doing something
in place of going to church. Unfortunately, Sunday has become
just another Saturday. What does the Bible say?

1. The commandment explained

Keeping God's Day happens to be the longest of the
Ten Commandments. (Exodus 20:8-11) When Jesus said
to put God and His Kingdom first, He also meant honoring
His Day.

2. The convictions experienced

The Pharisees had a list of 1,521 things that were not
allowed on the Sabbath. Most of them were ridiculous,

such as, killing a biting flea on the Sabbath would make you guilty of hunting.

3. The consecration expected

We are expected to surrender the Sabbath to God, to make it different than other days of the week. So what kinds of things are permissible on Sunday?

Let's make it a day of rest, since that's what "sabbath" means. I may need to go to the store or get gas on some Sundays, but I really do try to get it done by Saturday night.

Sunday is a great day to worship God, no matter what is happening in my life. Exiled to a rock island for his faith, John wrote, "I was in the spirit on the Lord's day." (Revelation 1:10)

We can serve God by serving others. Sunday is a good day to visit shut-ins, those in hospitals, or spend time with family.

When a little boy was asked to define "the Lord's Day," he answered, "It's a day to get acquainted with God." Well said! And Jesus said it well in Matthew 6:33.

As you pray today, ask God to show you
ways for you to keep His Day holy.

18

But seek ye first the kingdom of God,
and his righteousness; and all these things
shall be added unto you.
(Matthew 6:33, KJV)

God's Call

In *The Ministry of Shepherding,* Dr. Eugene Stowe
wrote, "Real shepherds are called, not hired ...
scriptural evidence is conclusive that the Christian ministry
must have its genesis in a definite, divine call."[1] Personally,
I have learned a few lessons about God's Call ...

1. God's Call begins with a growing awareness.

As Matthew 6:33 Christians, we only want God's
Will, and for some of us, that includes that special Call.
The prophet Jeremiah was called even before he was born.
(Jeremiah 1:5) There is usually a growing awareness before
an acknowledgement and acceptance. Dr. Stowe even said,
"the call should be so clear that the passage of time only
serves to amplify it."[2] My Call is as real today as it was
decades ago.

2. God's Call is the Call to preparation.

They used to say, "Open your mouth and God will fill
it!," but congregations these days are much too intelligent

for that. It's an awesome responsibility to preach God's Word, something for which I had to get a good education. I learned the first day in a college ministry class that "the Call to ministry is the Call to prepare."

3. God's Call can change forms.

My Call was very clear—to preach! I began as a youth pastor, then served as a weekend student-evangelist, and for more than three decades I've been a pastor. My Call is to preach, but one can preach while being used of God in more than one kind of ministry.

4. God's Call is God's Call.

For six months, I struggled. How could I be a preacher when I was too shy to even give a book report in high school? I then read about Moses in Exodus 4. He wasn't a good speaker either. His story became my story. It was never about me but it was all about God.

5. God's Call is to be answered.

After six months, I finally accepted God's Call. Could it be that God is calling you to something special in your Christian life? Preacher, missionary, teacher, doctor, lawyer, firefighter—whatever it is, it's time to accept that Call.

***

As you pray today, ask God to make His Call clear.

19

But strive first for the kingdom of God
and his righteousness, and all these things
will be given to you as well.
(Matthew 6:33, NRSV)

Living the Sanctified Life

In his book, *Returning to Your First Love,"* Dr. Tony
Evans wrote, "If you and I are going to keep our love
for Christ in first place where it belongs ... We are going
to have to learn how to live by the leading and direction of
the Holy Spirit rather than ... our flesh."[1]

There are good, biblical reasons for his statement:
"I know that nothing good dwells in me." (Romans 7:18)
"Those who are in the flesh cannot please God." (Romans
8:8) "Walk by the Spirit and you will not carry out the
desire of the flesh." (Galatians 5:16)

You may be thinking, "But this doesn't apply to me—
I'm saved!" So were the disciples, yet they had an ongo-
ing battle with the lack of trust and self-centeredness. Let's
look at the sanctified life from Galatians chapter 5 ...

1. Within everyone are desires of the flesh.

After we were saved, we probably did fine, for awhile.
Then there may have been a mistake, always followed by

guilt. "You were running well; who prevented you from obeying the truth?" (Galatians 5:7) Never our intention, but it happens.

2. There is a war raging inside.

"For the flesh lusts against the Spirit, and the Spirit against the flesh; and these are contrary to one another." (Galatians 5:17) There's a civil war going on within the heart of the unsanctified believer. The disciples were trying to meet their own needs instead of trusting God.

3. Learn how to starve the flesh.

In Galatians 5, Paul presents three categories of sin: Sexual sins (Galatians 5:19), superstitious sins (Galatians 5:20), and social sins (Galatians 5:20-21). We must boldly say, "Flesh, you are not going to eat today!"

4. Feed the Spirit.

"And those who are Christ's have crucified the flesh with its passions and desires. If we live in the Spirit, let us also walk in the Spirit." (Galatians 5:24-25)

In short, we live the sanctified life by seeking first the Kingdom of God and His righteousness. (Matthew 6:33)

As you pray today, ask God to sanctify you wholly, if you haven't already.

20

But seek first the kingdom of God and his righteousness,
and all these things will be added to you.
(Matthew 6:33, ESV)

Where Is God in Your Spiritual Life?

On a shelf in my study is a book by Dr. Richard Howard, *Where on Earth is God?* We would all agree that there are times in our lives when we tend to wonder.

But that's a two-way street! We can be so busy asking, "Where is God?," that we fail to realize He may be asking the same of us! Is God the center of my marriage? Is God involved in my decision making? Is God evident in other areas of my life? Christianity is supposed to be a personal Relationship with the King of kings. Once we are saved, we are no longer loners. We're all about Him and what He wants for us.

In Matthew 6:33, Jesus makes it clear that God is to be first above anyone and everything. With that in mind, let me ask you, "where is God" in your spiritual life?

As a pastor, I see too many Christians whose personal growth in Christ has come to a screeching halt! The Scripture says, "but as He who called you is holy, you also be holy in all your conduct." (1 Peter 1:15) The Christian life is not just a life of going to church—it's a life of holiness. It's striving to be more like Jesus every day of our lives.

While talking with the sales clerk at the mall, it came out that I was a pastor. As I was leaving, the salesman said, "Reverend, put in a good word for me with your Boss!" Unfortunately, that's the mentality of many people. To keep God first in my life, I must meet with Him, talk with Him, listen to Him, and no one can do it for me.

Only we can keep God first in our spiritual lives. We read in Luke 5:16, "So He Himself often withdrew into the wilderness and prayed." There's our Example. If the Sinless One felt the need to spend time alone with His Father on a regular basis, why shouldn't we?

As you pray today, ask God to show you ways to keep Him first in your spiritual life.

21

But seek first his kingdom and his righteousness,
and all these things will be given to you as well.
(Matthew 6:33, NIV)

Where Is God in Your Home?

The psalmist wrote, "Unless the LORD builds the house, They labor in vain who build it." (Psalm 127:1) In my opinion, most marital problems are due to selfishness. Each person in the relationship wants his or her own way, rather than the way of God. As a result, our homes are not built on firm foundations.

Two things are essential to every marriage, to every home, to every serious relationship …

1. Prayer

We've all heard it said, "A family that prays together, stays together." As a matter of fact, I grew up with those words in Old English hanging on our living room wall and embedded into my memory. A family altar is an absolute must in every household. In order to have a Matthew 6:33 home, a family must pray and have devotions together, even if just for a few moments a day.

Prayer is expected by Jesus Himself. More than once in Matthew chapter 6, Jesus doesn't say "If" you pray but He says "when" you pray and "when" you fast. It's just expected of a Christian!

2. Communication

It is imperative that a family be able to talk about anything. I think much of the success in raising our son is that Tommy knew he could come home from school and discuss anything without our being judgmental. No subject was off limits. Now he has a beautiful wife and a child of his own (with another on the way) and yet we still have lines of open communication, even if just by way of telephone.

Whenever I preach on the subject of the home and family, I usually tell our families to "turn the volume down" at their house!" The noise level is way too high in some households with arguing, TVs blaring, and the deafening silence of so many family members who have checked-out with their electronic devices. Why not explore options to bring everyone together under the same roof?

Let's put God first in our lives on a regular basis and that includes our home.

⋙⋯⋯⋯⋯⋯⋙⋯⋯⋯⋯⋘

As you pray today, ask God to help you
to create an atmosphere for worshiping
Christ in your home.

22

But seek first the kingdom of God and His righteousness,
and all these things shall be added to you.
(Matthew 6:33, NKJV)

Where Is God in Your Future?

When I was in high school, I had no clue as to what I would do for a career. All I wanted in high school was "out!" A buddy and I discovered that we were only two classes away from graduation, both of which were being offered in summer school. The school counselor reluctantly agreed to help us put it all into motion, allowing our graduation at the end of the summer following our junior year. That was back before students graduated early so we were not permitted to come back and walk with the class. We didn't care. They took us to the teacher's lounge and bought us king-sized bottles of Coca-Cola out of the machine, our reward for a concealed commencement.

Months later, feeling the need for some kind of beyond-high-school education, I attended Dekalb Tech, Atlanta Tech, and the Professional Academy of Commercial Art, where I experienced short-lived pursuits in auto mechanics and commercial art. During that time, I worked at Sears and as a freelance photographer. Finally, I decided to check in with God and seek what His Will might be for my life.

It's so easy to forget that God, in fact, has a plan for each of us. "For I know the plans I have for you …" (Jeremiah 29:11) What's after high school? Ask God! What's after college? Ask God! What's after that job offer? Ask God! What's in the future? Ask God!

If we will just inquire of God, He will direct us in the most perfect path according to His will. In the Scriptures we read, "Your ears shall hear a word behind you, saying, 'This is the way, walk in it,' Whenever you turn to the right hand Or whenever you turn to the left." (Isaiah 30:21) It's still important to listen for that still, small Voice.

Finding God in our future is going to require lots and lots of trust. It's the Matthew 6:33 way.

❖ ——————— ◆ ——————— ❖

As you pray today, ask God to reveal to you
more of His plan for your life.

23

Seek the Kingdom of God above all else, and live
righteously, and he will give you everything you need.
(Matthew 6:33, NLT)

Where Is God in Your
Problem-Solving?

Six-year old Harvey prayed, "Dear God, Charlie my
cat got run over and if You made it happen, You've
got to tell me why."[1] Little Harvey definitely had a problem. Ever been there?

What do you do when there's a problem at work? What
is your approach to a major catastrophe at home? How do
you get around a mountain in your path? Do you wring
your hands, worry, frantically search for a solution, or do
you take it to God? This is what Jesus is dealing with con-
cerning His disciples in Matthew 6:25-34. They were doing over-the-top worrying and Jesus was pointing them to
the only sensible solution: Seek God first.

The psalmist was clear: "I will lift up my eyes to the
hills—From whence comes my help? My help comes from
the LORD, Who made heaven and earth." (Psalm 121:1-
2) This is the passage I almost always read to patients just

before they go into surgery. Think about it: The same God Who created the entire universe is the One Who is going to be taking care of you today! That's encouraging!

The truth is, we usually end up going to Him anyway—as a last resort. The panic-stricken disciples did everything they knew to do in that sinking boat during a terrific storm. They were, after all, professional fishermen and experienced sailors. They no doubt cupped their hands and used whatever container that might have been on board to bail out the water. They probably lowered the sail and tried steering away from the winds, but when they realized this storm was no match, as a last resort, they finally went to Jesus.

The song writer put it this way ...

Oh, what peace we often forfeit,
Oh what needless pain we bear.
All because we do not carry
everything to God in prayer.

Got problems to solve? Why not go to Jesus and put God first in the problems of your life?

As you pray today, ask God to show you places in your life where you need to trust Him.

24

But seek ye first the kingdom of God,
and his righteousness; and all these
things shall be added unto you.
(Matthew 6:33, KJV)

First in Finance

After four years away from church, I was finally
saved at nineteen. Almost immediately, I thought
of storehouse tithing. Raised in a Christian home, my parents had taught me to tithe from my weekly allowance.

Barely still a teenager, I had several bills each month
that were overwhelming. A major department store had allowed me a credit card with which I had purchased clothes,
a stereo, and other items at a high rate of interest. Needless
to say, I had problems in the pocketbook!

In those days, I was employed by the Sears Catalog
Distribution Center near downtown Atlanta. Every other
Thursday was payday, but I never had enough money to
meet my monthly obligations. As a new Christian, however, I brought home my first paycheck, wrote out my tithe
check first, and placed it in the top drawer of my chest
of drawers. On Sunday, I put that check into the offering

plate. I remembered how Jesus told His disciples that if they put God first, He would meet their needs.

I was well aware of the Scripture: "'Bring all the tithes into the storehouse, That there may be food in My house, And try Me now in this,' Says the LORD of hosts, 'If I will not open for you the windows of heaven And pour out for you such blessing That there will not be room enough to receive it.'" (Malachi 3:10)

Though it felt good to tithe, the remaining 90% was just not enough to cover the bills that were due. I decided to write checks that were a little less than the amounts requested, but at least I was sending something and not ignoring my bills. I never heard a complaint and over time, God blessed my obedience.

Tips have increased to 15% and 20%, prices continue to rise, but God still only requires a tenth. Anything over that amount is beyond-the-tithe giving. Seeking God first means to keep God Number One in every area of our lives, even financially.

———————◈———————

As you pray today, ask God to help you take the steps to put Him first in your finances.

25

But strive first for the kingdom of God and his
righteousness,and all these things will be
given to you as well.
(Matthew 6:33, NRSV)

Facing Our Fears

When our son, Tommy, was a tiny tyke, he had trouble staying in his own bed at night. One evening, after a couple of trips to his bedroom to put him back in his own bed, I was exasperated. Sobbing, he blurted out, "I'm afraid of the dark!" Without thinking, I responded, "It's not the dark you should be afraid of—it's what's in the dark!" With one big wail, his feet pitter-pattered straight to our room, where he jumped into bed with his Mom. With a smile, Sandie's remark to me was, "Way to go, Sherlock!"

We all face some kind of fear. For some it's the fear of flying, for others, the fear of heights. Some even suffer from "frisbeetarianism," the fear that when you die, your soul goes up on the roof and stays there! The Bible is clear that we should never be frightened: "You shall not be afraid of the terror by night, Nor of the arrow that flies by day." (Psalm 91:5) When the disciples were afraid, Jesus pointed them toward their Creator. (Matthew 6:33) A few things to ponder ...

1. There is still a heavenly Father Who is at work in our lives.

God is aware and at work in you and me at all times. He knows what lies ahead and He knows all about your health, job, and your marriage. Jesus says there is no need for worry.

2. Worry is a slap in the Face of God.

Jesus was emphatic: "Quit your worrying!" (Matthew 6:25, 27, 28, 31, 34) The only thing anxiety will get us is an ulcer and an early grave!

3. The only way to learn to trust God is by trusting God.

I didn't learn to pastor out of a textbook—I learned from other preachers! I wasn't taught to preach in a classroom—I held weekend revivals and preached whenever the Lord presented the opportunity! To learn to trust God, we just need to start doing it! We will experience His Presence as we seek Him first.

<hr />

As you pray today, ask God to reveal your fears that need to be committed to Him.

26

But seek first the kingdom of God and his righteousness,
and all these things will be added to you.
(Matthew 6:33, ESV)

For the Birds!

In Matthew 6:25-34, the Greek verb for *"be anxious"* is used six times. Let's put this text in the context of what's happening …

1. Jesus was saddened by the pessimism.

We see in verse 25 that the disciples were worried. They were believers in God. They had not yet witnessed miracles at the hand of Jesus, but they had heard the stories of David and Goliath and Daniel in the lions' den. They had heard about Jonah, Noah, and the three Hebrew youths in a fiery furnace. They were aware of how the walls crumbled at Jericho and how fire fell on Carmel. They had anticipated the arrival of the Messiah and even believed that Jesus was the One, and yet they were still pessimistic.

2. The disciples were surrounded by the proof.

Verses 26-32 remind us that the birds are fed and the lilies are clothed. I've watched little birds hopping around on the ground and I haven't seen a scrawny one yet! They're all so plump and well-fed. Obviously, Someone is providing! People are the only ones not wise enough to trust God!

We are surrounded by proof everyday: The sun comes up every morning! Birds are fed, flowers are clothed! Cuts and scrapes on bodies heal! Tiny seeds turn into tall stalks of corn! The earth is just the right distance from the sun so we won't freeze or burn up!

3. We may be surprised by the prospect.

The promise of Christ is given in verses 33-34. *The Message* translates:

"Give your entire attention to what God is doing right now, and don't get worked up about what may or may not happen tomorrow."

You may be thinking, *"But you don't know what I'm facing!"* *"You don't know the news I just received!"* *"You don't know what I'm going through!"* *"You don't know, you have no idea ... "* No matter what's going on, Jesus still expects our complete trust! (v. 25a, 31a, 33-34a) It's not just for the birds!

❧ ⸺⸺ ◆ ⸺⸺ ☙

As you pray today, ask God to show you where you need to trust Him more.

27

But seek first his kingdom and his righteousness,
and all these things will be given to you as well.
(Matthew 6:33, NIV)

Following Jesus

Jesus said, "If anyone desires to come after Me, let him deny himself, and take up his cross daily, and follow Me." (Luke 9:23) The Greek word for *"follow"* is *"akoloutheo."* It is a verb, signifying action and it is also present tense, meaning action in progress with no sign of completion. It is active in voice, meaning the subject is the one doing the action. Being imperative, this is a command and because it's singular, we know we're talking about one person, very personal.

If we are to follow someone that way, it's extremely important to know who we're following! Since a kid, I've always loved helicopters. I once made a hospital call in Omaha, Nebraska. After my visit, I wondered about their helicopters, so I headed to the ER. As if I knew where I was going, I walked through the department then exited out the doors bearing a sign that read "NO RETURN." My thinking was that this exit would lead outside the

Emergency Room to the ambulances, and, oh yes, the helicopters.

Once outside, I looked around, and sure enough, there was a beautiful chopper parked not far away. Not only that, but there was a group of people gathered around it—a tour, and the pilot was pointing out various parts of the aircraft. This was my lucky day! I thought, "I'll go over and "blend-in" with the group and become part of the tour—no one will ever know!" As I got closer, however, I discovered that this was a group of girl scouts! Making a quick right, I walked along the wall down the ambulance driveway to the parking lot.

One cannot be a good leader until he or she becomes a good follower, but we also must be following the right One. Jesus said, "If anyone serves Me, let him follow Me; and where I am, there My servant will be also." (John 12:26) Following Jesus begins with putting Him first.

⚜————————◆————————⚜

As you pray today, ask God to show you
how you can become a better follower of Christ.

28

But seek first the kingdom of God and His righteousness,
and all these things shall be added to you.
(Matthew 6:33, NKJV)

Why Worry?

Americans have become specialists at worrying! As a matter of fact, I've heard that the term "Americanitis" has been ascribed to the rundown condition of nerves. One psychologist said, "Worry is the most subtle and destructive of all human diseases."

Although a negative practice, people worry daily—even Christians! And most of us fret over what never comes to pass! Some worry because it's a habit, like the elderly lady who remarked to her pastor one Sunday morning that she felt pretty good that day. But she then added, "I always feel bad when I feel good, because I am afraid I'm just going to feel worse!" The Bible has something to say about such a worrisome attitude …

1. The habit of worry is wrong!

Paul wrote the Philippians, "Don't worry about anything, instead, pray about everything." (Philippians 4:6, TLB) Worry is off-limits to the child of God! The word "worry" comes from a German term meaning, "to choke!" The habit of worry is choking the life out of us!

2. The cause of worry is fear!

We're all afraid of something! Children fear the dark, being left alone. Teens fear being different, rejected, and unaccepted. Young adults fear failure, finances. Parents fear responsibility, the future of their children. Middle-aged people fear work and the days ahead, while seniors fear health problems, loneliness, and death. Many just fear fear itself!

3. The opposite of worry is trust!

The only cure for worry is trust in God. One cannot trust God and worry at the same time! That's why there are 365 "fear nots" or "be not afraids" in the Bible, one for every day of the year!

The disciples were agonizing over their daily basic needs—food, clothes, shelter. Paul assured the believers at the church at Philippi, "And my God shall supply all your need according to His riches in glory by Christ Jesus." (Philippians 4:19) Therefore, the Lord Jesus asks His followers, including us, "Why worry?" (Matthew 6:33)

As you pray today, ask God to help you to trust Him with all of your concerns.

29

Seek the Kingdom of God above all else, and live
righteously, and he will give you everything you need.
(Matthew 6:33, NLT)

Faith

Yesterday we looked at the habit of worry. Worrying shows that one has "little faith" in what
God can do. By their continuous worrying, the disciples
of Jesus were indicating they did not have much faith in
their Teacher.

The writer to the Hebrews gives us a clear definition of
"faith." "Now faith is being sure of what we hope for and
certain of what we do not see. This is what the ancients
were commended for." (Hebrews 11:1-2, NIV) In that
same chapter, we have "God's Hall of Fame," a roster of the
names of men and women in the Bible who exercised great
faith in God. Each of them displayed for us …

1. Faith that's required.

For the Christian, faith is not optional, but required!
That's why the words *"faith"* and *"believe"* appear in the
New Testament almost 500 times! Without faith, we
cannot be saved, sanctified, grow spiritually, or even
please God!

2. Faith that's ridiculed.

I believe Noah was severely ridiculed for his unshakable faith in God. Until the flood, it had never rained and it took Noah 120 years to build that boat! They'll laugh at you if you're saved! They'll criticize you if you tithe! They'll call you "fanatic" if you pray for healing!

3. Faith that's risky.

Having no idea where they were going, many took risks! They scooted out on limbs of faith and trusted God, even when it made no sense.

4. Faith that's rugged.

The writer to the Hebrews speaks of how some believers were tortured, even sawn in two, all because of their extraordinary faith. Exercising faith is not always easy, but it's right.

5. Faith that's rewarded.

"But without faith it is impossible to please Him, for he who comes to God must believe that He is, and that He is a rewarder of those who diligently seek Him." (Hebrews 11:6) Why would we worry when we can trust and exercise tremendous faith in the One Who is faithful to us?

———

As you pray today, ask God to show
help you increase your faith.

30

But seek ye first the kingdom of God,
and his righteousness; and all these
things shall be added unto you.
(Matthew 6:33, KJV)

Following Jesus
All the Way Home

It was just a few weeks past little Lyric's six-month old birthday. Sandie and I were in California to visit our son, his wife, and our only grandbaby, Lyric Amerial. One day, while Tommy was on his job at Disneyland, the rest of us decided to go for a walk in their hilly La Habra neighborhood.

It was a nice trek halfway down the road, but our route home was pretty much uphill. Our kids are used to these early evening walks in the California hills, but Sandie and I are not, and it should be no surprise that we were lagging behind. Just as I made a joke about calling Tommy and having him pick me up on the curb at the next corner, Micha turned the stroller around to face us and began to pull our grandbaby backwards up the street. Focused on her grandparents, little Lyric began to laugh out loud. Sandie made the comment, "Well, I can make it now, if I just keep following that sweet smiling face all the way home!"

I thought, that's the Matthew 6:33 Christian life! If we'll just stay focused on the Face of Jesus and keep Him first in everything, we can follow Him all the way home, no matter how uphill the way becomes! The Scripture puts it this way: "Therefore we also, since we are surrounded by so great a cloud of witnesses, let us lay aside every weight, and the sin which so easily ensnares us, and let us run with endurance the race that is set before us, looking unto Jesus …" (Hebrews 12:1-2) That last phrase is the key to the entire passage, "looking unto Jesus." The NIV says, "Let us fix our eyes on Jesus."

Dr. Jack Graham reminds us, "Organize yourself according to seeking God's kingdom first. Matthew 6:33 promises that when we are faithful to tend to the work of God, he will be faithful to cause everything else to fall into place according to his very good plans for our lives."[1]

As you pray today, ask God to help you
to fix your eyes upon Jesus.

NOTES

INTRODUCTION

[1]Jack Graham, *Powering Up* (Wheaton, IL: Crossway Books, 2009), p. 204.

3—GOD FIRST!

[1]William M. Greathouse, *The Fullness of the Spirit* (Kansas City, MO: Beacon Hill Press, 1958), p. 9.

5—WORRIERS TO WEAPONS

[1]Earl Lee, *The Cycle of Victorious Living* (Kansas City, MO: Beacon Hill Press, 1971), p. 24.

9—"NO COWS IN TOMMY'S ROOM!"

[1]Randal Denny, *The Habit of Happiness* (Kansas City, MO: Beacon Hill Press, 1976), p. 12-13.

[2]Norman Vincent Peale, *The Power of Positive Thinking* (Upper Saddle River, NJ: Prentice-Hall, Inc., 1952), p. 122.

11—PUTTING GOD FIRST IN MY PRAYER LIFE

[1]Tony Evans, *Returning to Your First Love* (Chicago, IL, 1995), p. 77.

17—SUNDAY, STILL THE DAY OF THE LORD

[1]D.L. Moody, *Sabbath Living* http://sabbathliving.org/ sabbath-quotes (accessed 2017)

18—GOD'S CALL

[1]Eugene L. Stowe, *The Ministry of Shepherding* (Kansas City, MO: Beacon Hill Press, 1976), p. 15.

[2]Ibid, 16.

19—LIVING THE SANCTIFIED LIFE

[1]Tony Evans, *Returning to Your First Love* (Chicago, IL: Moody Press, 1995), p. 71.

23—WHERE IS GOD IN YOUR PROBLEM-SOLVING?

[1]Richard Howard, *Where on Earth is God?* (Kansas City, MO: Beacon Hill Press, 1983), p. 15.

30—FOLLOWING JESUS ALL THE WAY HOME

[1]Jack Graham, *Powering Up* (Wheaton, IL: Crossway Books, 2009), p. 204.